Some things are better left unsaid

Shreevalli Khaneja

BookLeaf Publishing

India | USA | UK

Presentation by *BookLeaf Publishing*

Web: www.bookleafpub.com

E-mail: info@bookleafpub.com

ISBN: 9789363319424

First edition 2024

I dedicate this to every over-thinker out there in the world. Every person who has struggled, who is struggling, you've got this. Don't give up, you're too good for that.....

ACKNOWLEDGEMENT

I would first off like to thank my parents, who forced me to get into reading (a hobby I now love), which has led me to expand my horizon and express myself openly through the manipulation of words. Thank you for helping me become the person I am today and the person I will be however many years down the line. I love you guys so so much, thanks for everything.

To my younger brother, you are annoying sure but I still love you. Thanks for making me an elder sister. Reach the stars and achieve so much, you got this kiddo.

To Tisya, the one who has been with me through so much. Though our friendship is relatively a short one, it feels to be decades old. You are basically my sister and I love how you haven't let go of my hand in the toughest of things. We might be miles apart, but I'm always here whenever you need me, just like you were.

To Vaishali, we have been friends for god knows how many years. It pains me that where we used

live seconds away, it now takes days to get there.
Thanks for being with me for all these years.

To Abdu, Riddhi, Fatma, and Uniza, we might
have met a few months ago but you guys have
now become my family away from home. Thank
you for making me feel loved and cared for. I
hope we stay like this for years to come. here's
to lot of new adventures and memories together.
Cheers!

To countless others who were a part of this
process, knowingly or unknowingly so, I thank
you. This wouldn't have been possible without
you.

Thank you from the bottom of my heart!

PREFACE

No one should possess the right to judge any person without having observed them from every lens available. When you try to talk to anyone, they say that they understand but sadly that's not the whole truth. They understand it based on the environment and society they grew up in and hence that understanding might hold no relevance in your case.

The thing is, people stigmatise topics and refuse to talk. They refuse in fear of being judged, in fear of standing out, fear of being called names. They take secrets to whatever comes after we die, saying not a word to the general masses. The emotions of a human are an ever-tangled string, a puzzle that has no definite solution.

But the heartbreaking truth is that parents pressurise their children, kids pressurise their peers, teens pressurise themselves and unknowingly succumb to it, destroying themselves. Parents lie to their kids to protect their innocence and kids lie to keep that image. They suffer and find themselves hanging off a ledge, looking upon the abyss of worst case scenarios. They end up anxious, depressed, traumatised or dealing with other such pain in the ass conditions. While many find the strength to pull themselves back to stable ground, so many give up and end up falling deep into the endless pit.

Growing up is the hardest phase of life only people tend to forget how hard it is. it is cardinal to not lose hope in this time frame because even when the Sun plays hide and seek behind the clouds, it is required to reveal itself eventually.

I may not know a lot about parenting, but I do know this. Having friends who came face to face with the demons of betrayal and were left alone, and having dealt with it myself, with no support or comfort, it pains to become one with the shadows. It hurts to be left alone in a foreign place. It hurts to be forsaken by those you trust. There are days where i feel no reason to make an effort but there are also days when I am perfectly aware of my capability to change things for the better.

When you experience certain things, the voices in your head grow loud, disturbing you day and night and it takes all of you to keep them at bay. The podcast of curiosity, demons, epiphanies

and a bunch of other things becomes the
background music to our essence of being.

I bring this collection to you, a bunch of my
thoughts that give you an insight into the mind
of an over-thinker and the chaos that brings in
my day to day. Hopefully this give a bit more
weight to the title of the book,

Some things are better left unsaid.

July 2024

The Art of Arrangement

Stars aligned,
constellations created,
and yet there are wonderers
who question how people
can see meaning
in a handful of stars.

Flowers arranged,
bouquets are made,
and yet there are questioners
who ask how people
comprehend a message
in a mere bunch of flowers.

Cloth sewn,
costumes take shape,
and yet there are critics
who challenge the creator,
their intentions and ask
how meaning be seen in stitches.

Machines assembled,
creations take birth,
and yet there are tinkerers
who critique the maker

asking how this helps,
what purpose does it serve.

Feel

I feel sick
Sick with myself
Sick of everything
I wanna hurt myself
Have it physically manifest
But I don't think i should
Im trouble
You decide good or bad
I sit here
Holding in my tears
A wet waterline
But don't break the dam
They cant fall through
I'll worry everyone
Im trouble again
Beyond repair
Like an opened stitch
Easy fix to be fair
When you ask for the thread
Thats what scares me
The asking for help
Its not something i want to do
Because that just reminds me
And confirms my fear
That I'm trouble again

Curiosity

What is the thing that caught my eye
Causing the gears of my brain to turn
What is this feeling i experience
I feel my stomach churn
Lost in a sea of questions
I give in to this wanderlust
This journey that i hope will give me answers
Scurrying around, in my mind
Are random thoughts and interesting finds
Encyclopaedias won't quench
My never ending thirst
The questions i ask
Cannot be found in books
They're in-conventional to some
Common for other people
But know that your curiosity is valid
Thats how you grow into who you are

Desperate

I wait for responses
I wait for your calls
But what do i get in return?
Silence. Cruel, ringing silence
They say silence is sweet
But is it really
Doesn't it make you question
What is wrong with you
What did you do to deserve this
I guess i might be a special case
Questioning my very essence
Should i change?
Why am i like this
Is this why people
Distance themselves from me
Leave me behind
As i wait for them to turn back
To give some closure
Some sort of explanation
Behind their actions and intentions
Was i not good enough
Am i not good enough
I am desperate for a word
Even if its not a compliment
At least you acknowledge my existence
The fact that i meant something

Whats the point

Whats the point of taking my name
When my work is not valued
What is the point in including me
When you don't want me as a part of
The work at hand, the task initiated
Is it only because they know my name
Because I am known to the masses
You give me position it means something
But what would it be, if i am not valued
If i am not respected enough
To actually be approached with the work
Why am i here, if you don't want me
Do you just need me, my recognition
As a means to show that you do something
When the truth is the complete opposite?

Words

Words heal and words break
A couple of words, strong enough to terminate
Words sharp, blade of a knife missed narrow
Words blunt, force of a piercing arrow
Words healing, the almighty cure
Words sealing, the promise secure
Words destructive, unthinkably cataclysmic
Words nuclear, causing activity seismic
Words simpler, clear as a crystal ball
Words complex, meant to make ur skin crawl

Shift

Something has changed
In the past few sun sets and rises
the emotional burden
but really just unsaid compromises
they come they go
new faces in the mix
my gut warns me to be wary
a situation at hand to fix
Is it my place to have a say
I don't want to overstep
This shift in perspectives
An off beat step
reading into it too much maybe
can't really tell
I don't like the way its changed
doesn't sit well
They're harmless right?
what could they possibly do
i try to convince myself
but catch me doubting it too
Wish I could bury myself away
the negativity at least
something about it reminds
me of an unhinged beast
feels like a break

an abyss is forming within me
can't really tell
If i want them to see
Thats the problem
i want to say a word
but also not, honestly
because its more of a sword
some wounds run deep
some never really heal
this could turn into one of those
unless I suppress and don't feel
This shouldn't affect me
not this bad really
But I see physical changes
holding unsettling familiarity

Caged

Tears drop from my eyes
Blood seeps thru the open scars
Scars hidden by tough skin
Taking emotions as the drops fall
Drop by drop i loose my smile
Loose the little faith in life
Loose the will to even try
What is the point of this cycle
The never ending journey i ask
I ask myself why don't i end it
Why don't I have the courage too
Its not cowardice holding me back
Its my honour my word to them
Dreams of a carefree child
Dreams i wanna fulfil
I want to give my hundred percent
Yet invisible chains bind me
Something stops me from doing it
All i do is stare into the unknown
If confrontation worked
My walls would have shattered
Burnt to ashes long ago
But those confronting words do nothing
Except reopen already healing scars
To them, we are careless, completely naive

But in true fashion, we are explosives
Live wires that can trigger any moment
If opening up was an option
And honesty was really the best policy
I would not have to carry
An invisible baggage of pain
Keeping my secrets, silencing myself
Keeping quiet because my input was deemed
unnecessary
Confidence is a mask, hiding me behind
The broken child who never really lived
The maturity that came before it should have
The harsh cold reality of our society
Is that emotions make you weak
But emotionless people are called insane
Loving people are scarce
Invasive people one too many
You cry, you are a crybaby
You speak loudly, you are rude
You try to stay quiet, you're urged to speak up
And as soon as you do you're shut down
This god awful generation gap
And how they have only one thing to blame
The one thing that holds my sanity
Is called useless if I don't satisfy them
You make an error, your faults are called out
You try a trend, now you are doing it for clout
Things would have been so much simpler
If these demons found new residence

Because apparently I unknowingly
Put my mind up on the market for sale
I loose myself drop by drop
Internally crying in agony
But the painful words have numbed me so
I barely feel a smidgen of pain
Malice is long forgotten
Happiness is now a luxury
The rare moments i do feel content
Then they say whats wrong the other day you
were happy
All I can do now is
Walk with my head held high
Fake it till you make it
Seems like the only route to survive
Hopefully a day comes
Where i let go of this load
But as of today, as of now
I sit here, in a little cage
A dragon with its wings cut off

Comparison of life

Do you ever think
How they must feel?
Those who work hard all day,
To eat two square meals.
Do you ever wonder,
What the rich ones do?
To reach the place they hold today,
The struggles they've been through
Do you not feel curious?
To know the problems faced,
By the kids of the new generation,
When life goes at such a pace.
Don't you want to ask,
The people who are insecure?
What is it that makes them like this,
What makes them so unsure?
Have you ever felt
The dire need to ask
Those few ambitious dreamers,
Who shape life like hot glass?
Struggles are different for people
And achievements vary also.
It will probably be better
If we stop comparing lives so.

Drifting apart

We used to play together
Galavanting around the locality
Our troop of soldiers
Fighting the arms of the clock
Just to play and be free a moment longer
To have a sense of control
But that was years ago
No one roams, no one is careless
We don't fight the hourglass anymore
The sand falls away and we take no notice
The wanderlust has wandered off
Materialistic things now matter more
Followers and views on the social feed
Defines who you have a relationship with
The ladder of status has finally appeared
People take their places on the steps
Hoping that the rush pushes them further up
And praying they don't slip
Old bonds are in tatters,
Newer bonds are oh so weak
Trust is hard to find and so is authenticity
You never can tell what is running
Behind those calculated moves
The true intentions behind interactions
Remain hidden in crevices of requests

The world has changed to be a new place
Our interactions have changed alongside
Although i really wish
Those bonds, cannot be smelted back

Walls of Glass

Walls built around me
Encaging me in glass
Though fragile, it comes crashing
And nicks me in uncountable places
Sitting in the depths of night
Tracing patterns into a mosaic of cuts
Incomparably beautiful but painfully so
Scars are indeed breath-taking
The bruises and blood is unseen
Others may see me to be perfectly fine
That only means that I held myself
and hid my pain, buried into the void of me
Those walls have been built fresh
but the glass seems to be tinted
It feels like calm before the storm
The next explosion will not be the last

By our side

They call us best friends
But they can't act like that
You call them your everything
But it doesn't work like that
They are there for you
The guiding light, the north star
And they will accompany you
But they can only come so far
One day you'll loose them
It will all burn to ashes
That day is when you stand
Alone to face the masses
Learn from them but dont forget
To learn from life too
They make errors and they can misguide
They are human just like me and you
Google maps isn't always correct
Siri doesn't have all the solutions
Cherish this procedure of trial and error
That ties together this relation
Maybe they don't get you sometimes
Understandable, they grew up different
You worry about games and hangouts
They had to worry about what career meant
Life back then was hard

But it is harder today
The competition between us only
Get complicated day by day
As the day passes through
As the moon takes its turn
A single thought comes to mind
A lantern continually burns
They can share their knowledge
Whats makes their foundation
We can only build further on it
Life doesn't have the option of evasion
Troubles come and go
Thats the way life works
But they are always by our side
Even when we might be something of a jerk
They deserve so much more
They are the ones who are unrecognised
There is nothing we can't do
When we have them by our side

Expectations

I got excited when i saw you typing
Thinking what it would be this time
Now i regret setting high expectations
Because you just wanted to cut off our ties
I sit here and ponder what went askew
But you took that step, what can i even do
People ask me, how i stay strong
How is it possible my mask stays on
Well, after years of practice
It's like you've had it since you are born

Cold

The blizzard of thoughts inside
Because i have no one to share with
My trusted comrades,
The keepers of my secrets
Seem to have vanished
What wrong did i do
They left me this way
In the middle of an intersection
To choose my own path forward
Those i called my own
No longer acknowledge my existence
It feels cold inside me
A numbness locks it into my being
Thoughtless i stand in the middle
Waiting for someone to find me

My Conscience

Even in a secluded corner
I am not alone
I have someone with me
I have my conscience
I have my thoughts for company
They never really visit much
But now they appear
Not hesitating
A voice in my mind
Tells it to me straight
What it thinks
Of my very existence
That voice, tho comforting
Is not very positive
Its comforting pain
Pain brought by memories
Pain brought by words
Like a numbness
That blocks the sting of the blade
Yet helps release the anxiousness
That had been bottled up
Like a scroll in the ocean of syllables
Riding the currents
But then it reminds me
Of the good times

That came after the struggle
The light that i found
After the curtain had been lifted
I saw within myself
Cherishing the company
Even if they were not there in front of me
They still were a part of me
And leave me with a discovery
I am never alone
There are always two of us
Me and My Conscience

Comforting

A cup of coffee holds comfort
That I would want from a hug
A simple conversation reminds me
of people waiting to listen to what I say
A quiet moment makes me reminisce
about stolen moments of silence
A dark room reminds me
of freedom from being judged at all

Mistakes

24

I know I have made a mistake
What that was, I don't really know
I know it's hard to reach my dreams
Why it's become harder is something I can't spell
I know it's hard to trust someone
But why is it that way, I don't know
I take myself to be a burden, I know that
A burden on whom, my heart won't tell

Issues

I want to tell
But I'd rather not
Spell out the problem
But hide it as well
I don't wanna be trouble
But want them to hear me out
I don't wanna annoy them
But want to reach out
Don't want to be a burden
But need them for support
It's a fine line to walk
One side wanting help
Other, assuming they don't care
Don't want to give them
More stuff on their plate
Want to forget the fact that
I'm an annoyance at best
The thing is I know
I know they won't mind me sharing
But it's my anxiety talking
It makes me into something else
Something I'd rather not be
I want to tell the ones who already know
Tell them it's happening again
But the same reason I stop

I don't wanna trouble them
It's stupid you're probably thinking
Well I know it sounds like that
But it's a real crisis to me
Hitting whenever and wherever
I struggle to communicate
But seem to have a way with words
I love to tease them and sit with them
But hiding the truth hurts
I honestly think of myself as a burden
A problem they have to deal with
Whenever I have an anxiety issue
That's who I replace myself with
The usual me doesn't care
Knowns people will say something if thats the
case
The anxiety me is a little shitty
Loves to rub that thought in my face